Poems of Light

Other Books by Carl Japikse:

The Tao of Meow
The Hour Glass
The Light Within Us
Pigging Out in Columbus
Teeing Off in Central Ohio
Breaking 80

with Robert R. Leichtman, M.D.:

The Art of Living (5 volumes)
The Life of Spirit (3 volumes)
Books of Light

Poems of Light

Edited by Carl Japikse

Enthea Press
Columbus, Ohio

The artwork on the cover is *The Architect's Dream* (1830) by Thomas Cole (1801-1848). It is reproduced here courtesy of the Toledo Museum of Art in Toledo, Ohio.

POEMS OF LIGHT
Copyright © 1991 by Carl Japikse

All Rights Reserved. No part of this book may be used or reproduced in any manner whatsoever without written permission, except in the case of brief quotes embodied in articles and reviews. Printed in the United States of America. Direct all inquiries to: Enthea Press, P.O. Box 249, Canal Winchester, Ohio 43110.

ISBN 0-89804-156-2

Contents

Introduction   9
Poems of Light   13
The Presence of God   14
    Elysium   15
    The Crannied Wall   16
    Here in the Self   17
    Life's Mystery   18
    Verses from The Rubáiyát   21
    The Outer and the Inner   22
    The Coming Glory of the Light   23
    Immanence   24
    Transcendence   24
    Omnipresence   25
Our Response   26
    My Heart Leaps Up   27
    Out in the Fields with God   28
    Music   29
    The End of Being   30
    The World is Too Much With Us   31
    Pan With Us   32
    Finite and Infinite   34
    The Pilgrim   35
    The Little Tippler   36
    Today   37

Creeds   38
   Grand is the Seen   39
   The Bohemian Hymn   40
   To Althea, from Prison   41
   A Creed   43
   The Universal Prayer   45
   Going To Church   47
   Pippa's Song   48
   The Problem   49
Transformation   52
   Alchemy   53
   Merlin   54
   I Ponder'd in Silence   58
   A Prayer in Spring   59
   A Phantom of Delight   60
   The Symbolic and the Real   62
   Thought   63
   A Sonnet   65
   Brahma   66
   The Trial by Existence   67
   The Overheart   70
   Revelation   73
Divine Life and Laws   74
   Light Shining Out of Darkness   75
   Theophany   76
   Life's Reverberation   77
   Shoestring   78

    The Informing Spirit   79
    Song of the Universal   80
    An Essay on Man   83
    The Calming Thought of All   89
Inspiration   90
    Preface to Endymion   91
    Genius   93
    Eidólons   94
    Pound for Pound   98
    For That I Came   99
    The Genius of the Place   100
    Inspiration   102
    More Fragments From the Rubiáyát   103
    Aurora Leigh   104
    Synthesis   109
Death   110
    The Unknown Region   111
    Can This Be Death?   112
    After Death in Arabia   113
    Under the Light   116
    Sevens   117
    Ozymandias   118
    Sail Out For Good, Eidólon Yacht!   119
    Rima   120
    The Windhover   121
    Death   122
    Joy, Shipmate, Joy!   123

Visions   124
   Here on Earth   125
   On First Looking Into Chapman's Homer   126
   Dirt   127
   The Clod and the Pebble   129
   Ode   130
   Koh-i-Noor   138
   The World's All Right   139
   The Divine Image   142
   The Base of All Metaphysics   143
   Renewal   144

Introduction

Day breaks every morning, in every part of the world. We count on it. We take it for granted. We would panic if the sun did not rise some day.

Light dawns in human consciousness on a regular basis, too. Perhaps not every morning, at least as we reckon the day—but often enough that we ought to sit up and take notice. But we don't. We take it for granted.

There are many ways light tries to break into our minds and hearts—and guide our lives. The music of a Wagner, Beethoven, or Bach is light translated into sound. The majestic art of a Rembrandt or a Thomas Cole is light expressed as color and shade. The electrifying brilliance of a scientific genius such as Nikola Tesla is light brought forth as—well, light.

One of the purest ways in which light enters the human imagination and becomes a part of its values, principles, and character, though, is through inspired poetry. In the days of Arthur—and King Arthur was a historical figure, even though he has been eclipsed by his mythological counterpart—poets were held in awe, as though they were magicians. That, after all, is who Merlin was—Myrddin, an epic poet who sang the praises of Arthur. Over the years, our human imagination turned him into Merlin the magician. But both the real man and the mythical hero dealt with light.

Not all poetry is filled with light, of course. But when poetry realizes all that it can be, when it reaches its highest, most ethereal state, then it is the closest thing to light we can experience. At this level, poetry is like the earliest rays of dawn streaming forth from the Pierian Spring—the home of the Muses on Mt. Olympus. By reading enlightened poetry, we, too, can commune with the nectar and ambrosia of its original inspiration.

The purpose of this collection is to draw forth and present in a single collection some of the most outstanding examples of enlightened poetry in the English language. Some of the pieces will be familiar ones, but many will be unknown to you, unless you are already a connoisseur of poetry. In fact, some of the poets included may be a surprise—because their reputations have been colored and restricted by other poems that are more well known.

Alexander Pope, for instance, is often thought to be a spiteful curmudgeon who wrote clever satires at the expense of other people. In point of fact, he wrote some of the most inspired poems in the English language—in particular, *The Essay on Man,* an epic of the relationship of man and God. This poem has no equal in the English language. Unfortunately, it is too long to reproduce in an anthology of this kind in its entirety, but I have included two lengthy excerpts.

Elizabeth Barrett Browning is renowned for her *Sonnets to the Portuguese*—yet all but unrecognized for her exquisite spiritual verse. I have included several sonnets by her, plus a long excerpt from her epic poem on human creativity and love, *Aurora Leigh.*

When John Masefield was poet laureate of England, he was thought of mostly as a poet of the sea, somewhat out of step with modern times. Perhaps the critics of that day were out of step with Masefield, however; he wrote some of the most thoughtful verse of this century dealing with the inner life.

Other poets featured in this collection include Walt Whitman, Robert Frost, and Emily Dickinson. In addition, there are many selections by other, less-well-known poets.

The one thing all of these poems have in common is the measure of light they radiate. These poets did not just have *insight* into the nature of divine life; they had *vision* as well. By this I mean they had the ability to take their insights and embody them in words in such a way that the reader can be led to similar insights as well.

This is the dynamic nature of light as it is expressed through poetry. The good poet becomes a vehicle through which thousands, perhaps millions, of readers can in turn be illumined, as they read these poems on their own and respond to them.

As you read them, let your imagination and your mind be stretched. It is not the goal of these poems to reinforce old prejudices and thought habits. On the contrary, they are deliberately written to shake up the old grey matter and help you look at life from a different, more spiritual perspective. When Emily Dickinson proclaims that she has been struck by lightning, for example, she does not mean this literally. She means she has been struck by bolts of light—the raw force of inspiration.

As you allow yourself to be the targets of these bolts, it will be important to do more with it than just watch your hair stand on end. We must let the light within the poems guide us to new understanding, deeper comprehension, and an overall awakening of our spiritual nature. We must have the courage to expand our awareness, challenge and discard old thought habits, and establish new ways of acting. We must learn to love, even as God loves us. We must learn patience, even as God is patient with us. We must learn joy, so we can share in God's joy and celebration.

Not all poets are enlightened, of course—or even good visionaries. Many are bogged down excessively in their private hurts and agonies, and never leap up to the higher level of consciousness where they can be properly inspired. Such poets cannot inspire us to our own deeper understanding and commitment. But this does not diminish the value or impact of the poems collected here.

Nor are these the only spiritual poems the English

language has produced. These are just a few of the many excellent poems these poets—and others—have produced. If you find these poems as inspiring and enlightening as I have, I hope you will seek out other selections by these same writers.

It will be worth your trouble.

—Carl Japikse

Poems of Light

The Presence of God

The most fundamental kind of spiritual poem is that of awakening and discovery—awakening to the reality of divine life and discovery that God is, indeed, present everywhere and in everything. While science still struts about, thinking itself important because it has not yet officially decided if God exists, poets are light years ahead. The fact of God is not a mystery; it is a demonstrated reality. Anyone with half a wit can prove the reality of God in less than five minutes, if he cares to use his intelligence. The only mysteries of life are 1) why more people have not come to realize the presence of God in their lives, and 2) why they have not yet figured out what they are supposed to do with it once they discover it.

These poems may help stir your understanding.

Elysium
by Emily Dickinson

Elysium is as far as to
The very nearest room,
If in that room a friend await
Felicity or doom.

What fortitude the soul contains
That it can so endure
The accent of a coming foot,
The opening of a door!

The presence of Light is our proof of heaven. It is truly no further than the very nearest room—the kingdom of heaven is at hand. Let's open the door.

The Crannied Wall
by Alfred Lord Tennyson

Flower in the crannied wall,
I pluck you out of the crannies,
I hold you here, root and all, in my hand,
Little flower—but *if* I could understand
What you are, root and all, and all in all,
I should know what God and man is.

> *If we could understand why flowers grow in crannies, we could understand why we get stuck in odd corners and the cracks of life as well. It's not that hard to understand, either—if we have a will to know.*

Here in the Self
by John Masefield

Here in the self is all that man can know
Of Beauty, all the wonder, all the power,
All the unearthly color, all the glow,
Here in the self which withers like a flower;
Here in the self which fades as hours pass,
And droops and dies and rots and is forgotten,
Sooner, by ages, than the mirroring glass
In which it sees its glory still unrotten.
Here in the flesh, within the flesh, behind,
Swift in the blood and throbbing on the bone,
Beauty herself, the universal mind,
Eternal April wandering alone.
The god, the holy ghost, the atoning lord,
Here in the flesh, the never yet explored.

Life's Mystery
by Elizabeth Barrett Browning

We sow the glebe, we reap the corn,
    We build the house where we may rest,
And then, at moments, suddenly
We look up to the great wide sky,
Inquiring wherefore we were born,
    For earnest or for jest?

The sense folding thick and dark
    About the stifled soul within,
We guess diviner things beyond,
And yearn to them with yearning fond;
We strike out blindly to a mark
    Believed in, but not seen.

We vibrate to the pant and thrill
    Wherewith Eternity has curled
In serpent-twine about God's seat:
While, freshening upward to his feet,
In gradual growth his full-leaved will
    Expands from world to world.

And, in the tumult and excess
    Of act and passion under sun,
We sometimes hear—oh, soft and far,
As silver star did touch with star,
The kiss of Peace and Righteousness
    Through all things that are done.

God keeps his holy mysteries
    Just on the outside of man's dream;

In diapason slow, we think
To hear their pinions rise and sink,
While they float pure beneath his eyes,
    Like swans adown a stream.

Abstractions, are they, from the forms
    Of his great beauty?—exaltations
From his great glory?—strong previsions
Of what we shall be?—intuitions
Of what we are—in calms and storms
    Beyond our peace and passions?

Things nameless! which, in passing so,
    Do stroke us with a subtle grace;
We say, "Who passes?"—they are dumb,
We cannot see them go or come,
Their touches fall soft, cold, as snow,
    Upon a blind man's face.

Yet, touching so, they draw above
    Our common thoughts to Heaven's unknown;
Our daily joy and pain advance
To a divine significance
Our human love—O mortal love,
    That light is not its own!

And sometimes horror chills our blood
    To be so near such mystic Things,
And we wrap round us for defense
Our purple manners, moods of sense—
As angels from the face of God
    Stand hidden in their wings.

Poems of Light — 20

And sometimes through life's heavy swound
    We grope for them, with strangled breath
We stretch our hands abroad and try
To reach them in our agony;
And widen, so, the broad life-wound
    Soon large enough for death.

> *It's only our dulled senses which keep these intuitions from being more real in our lives. Nor do we have to wait upon death for a clearer understanding; if we ask, it will be given us; if we seek, we shall find.*

Verses from The Rubáiyát
by Omar Khayyám, as translated by Edward Fitzgerald

Wake! For the Sun, who scatter'd into flight
The Stars before him from the Field of Night,
    Drives Night along with them from Heav'n,
        and strikes
The Sultan's Turret with a Shaft of Light.

Before the phantom of False morning died,
Methought a Voice within the Tavern cried,
    "When all the Temple is prepared within,
Why nods the drowsy Worshipper outside?"

Not because he's tired from trying too hard!

The Outer and the Inner
by Emily Dickinson

The Outer from the Inner
Derives its Magnitude—
'Tis Duke, or Dwarf, according
As is the Central Mood;

The fine, unvarying Axis
That regulates the Wheel,
Though Spokes spin more conspicuous
And fling a dust the while.

The Inner paints the Outer,
The Brush without the Hand,
Its Picture publishes precise,
As is the inner Brand.

On fine Arterial Canvas
A Cheek, perchance a Brow,
The Star's whole Secret in the Lake
Eyes were not meant to know.

The Coming Glory of the Light
by Edwin Arlington Robinson

I cannot find my way: there is no star
In all the shrouded heavens anywhere;
And there is not a whisper in the air
Of any living voice but one so far
That I can hear it only as a bar
Of lost, imperial music, played when fair
And angel fingers wove, and unaware,
Dead leaves to garlands where no roses are.

No, there is not a glimmer, nor a call,
For one that welcomes, welcomes when he fears,
The black and awful chaos of the night;
For through it all—above, beyond it all—
I know the far-sent message of the years,
I feel the coming glory of the Light!

Immanence
by Richard Hovey

Enthroned above the world although he sit,
Still is the world in him and he in it;
    The self-same power in yonder sunset glows
That kindled in the words of Holy Writ.

Transcendence
by Richard Hovey

Though one with all that sense or soul can see,
Not imprisoned in his own creations, he,
    His life is more than stars or winds or angels—
The sun doth not contain him nor the sea.

Omnipresence
by Edward Everett Hale

A thousand sounds, and each a joyful sound;
The dragon flies are humming as they please,
The humming birds are humming all around,
The clithra all alive with buzzing bees,
Each playful leaf its separate whisper found,
As laughing winds went rustling through the grove;
And I saw thousands of such sights as these,
And heard a thousand sounds of joy and love.

And yet so dull I was, I did not know
That He was there who all this love displayed,
I did not think how He who loved us so
Shared all my joy, was glad that I was glad;
And all because I did not hear the word
In English accents say, "It is the Lord."

It is on the wavelengths of love, joy, peace, and wisdom that we commune with God. Our fears, worries, ignorance, and greed cut off the communion. The loss is ours.

Our Response

Establishing the fact of the presence of God is not nearly as important as deciding how we will respond to this certain knowledge.

Some people would teach us that faith and belief are the correct responses. Faith and belief are indeed important, but mostly so that we can learn to take our first, trembling steps toward a more mature response. In any event, we should never believe that our full response to God's life and purpose should stop with faith. It must go on to include:

Compassion.
Joy.
Forgiveness.
Optimism.
Commitment.
Peace.
Integrity.
Generosity.

And above all, wisdom. For this is what light is, the love and wisdom of God that shines through our life, as we express it through our work, character, and dreams.

It is only at great peril that we respond to the fact of God with rebelliousness, self-centeredness, ignorance, and greed. These are flaws that keep us from responding fully; they cripple us and leave us contained within our own dense shell. No, we must rise above the material aspects of life and learn to respond to God fully and continuously, as though the divine life were a constant and complete part of ourselves, and we a part of it.

My Heart Leaps Up
by William Wordsworth

My heart leaps up when I behold
    A rainbow in the sky;
So was it when my life began;
So is it now I am a man;
So be it when I shall grow old,
    Or let me die!
The Child is Father of the Man;
And I could wish my days to be
Bound each to each by natural piety.

> *Each of us develops our own response mechanism; perhaps it is a rainbow, perhaps it is a jet plane soaring into the sky. We need to nurture and broaden this response mechanism so that it is constantly attuned to the vitality and purpose of God.*

Out in the Fields with God
by Elizabeth Barrett Browning

The little cares that fretted me
    I lost them yesterday,
Among the fields above the sea,
    Among the winds at play.
Among the lowing of the herds,
    The rustling of the trees,
Among the singing of the birds,
    The humming of the bees.

The foolish fears of what might happen,
    I cast them all away
Among the clover-scented grass,
    Among the new-mown hay,
Among the husking of the corn,
    Where drowsy poppies nod
Where ill thoughts die and good are born—
    Out in the fields with God.

Music
by Ralph Waldo Emerson

Let me go where'er I will
I hear a sky-born music still:
It sounds from all things old,
It sounds from all things young,
From all that's fair, from all that's foul,
Peals out a cheerful song.

It is not only in the rose,
It is not only in the bird,
Not only where the rainbow glows,
Nor in the song of woman heard,
But in the darkest, meanest things
There alway, alway something sings.

'Tis not in the high stars alone,
Nor in the cup of budding flowers,
Nor in the red-breast's mellow tone,
Nor in the bow that smiles in showers.
But in the mud and scum of things
There alway, alway something sings.

When He was done, God labeled all of creation good. We are the ones who insist on seeing certain things and events as mud and scum, to our own detriment.

The End of Being
by Seneca, translated by H.C. Leonard

The end of being is to find out God!
And what is God? A vast almighty Power
Great and unlimited, whose potent will
Brings to achievement whatsoe'er He please.
He is all mind. His being is infinite—
All that we see and all that we do not see.
The Lord of heaven and earth, the God of Gods.
Without Him nothing is. Yet what He is
We know not! When we strive to comprehend
Our feeble guesses leave the most concealed.
To Him we owe all good we call our own.
To Him we live, to Him ourselves approve.
He is a friend forever at our side.
What cares He for the bleeding sacrifice?
O purge your hearts and lead the life of good!
Not in the pride of temples made with stone
His pleasure lies, but in the piety
Of consecrated hearts and lives devout.

The World is Too Much With Us
by William Wordsworth

The world is too much with us; late and soon,
Getting and spending, we lay waste our powers:
Little we see in Nature that is ours;
We have given our hearts away, a sordid boon!
This Sea that bares her bosom to the moon;
The winds that will be howling at all hours,
And are up-gathered now like sleeping flowers;
For this, for every thing, we are out of tune;
It moves us not.—Great God! I'd rather be
A Pagan suckled in a creed outworn;
So might I, standing on this pleasant lea,
Have glimpses that would make me less forlorn;
Have sight of Proteus rising from the sea;
Or hear old Triton blow his wreathèd horn.

Divine force answers to many names. Some are Christian, some are not. No honest attempt to commune with God is ever pagan, so long as it brings light into the physical plane.

Pan With Us
by Robert Frost

Pan came out of the woods one day—
His skin and his hair and his eyes were gray,
The gray of the moss of walls were they—
    And stood in the sun and looked his fill
    At wooded valley and wooded hill.

He stood in the zephyr, pipes in hand,
On a height of naked pasture land;
In all the country he did command
    He saw no smoke and he saw no roof.
    That was well! and he stamped a hoof.

His heart knew peace, for none came here
To this lean feeding, save once a year
Someone to salt the half-wild steer,
    Or homespun children with clicking pails
    Who see so little they tell no tales.

He tossed his pipes, too hard to teach
A new-world song, far out of reach,
For a sylvan sign that the blue jay's screech
    And the whimper of hawks beside the sun
    Were music enough for him, for one.

Times were changed from what they were:
Such pipes kept less of power to stir
The fruited bough of the juniper
    And the fragile bluets clustered there
    Than the merest aimless breath of air.

They were pipes of pagan mirth,
And the world had found new terms of worth.
He laid him down on the sunburned earth
    And raveled a flower and looked away.
    Play? Play?—What should he play?

Finite and Infinite
by Elizabeth Barrett Browning

The wind sounds only in opposing straits,
The sea, beside the shore; man's spirit rends
Its quiet only up against the ends
Of wants and oppositions, loves and hates,
Where, worked and worn by passionate debates,
And losing by the loss it apprehends,
The flesh rocks round and every breath it sends
Is ravelled to a sigh. All tortured states
Suppose a straitened place. Jehovah Lord,
Make room for rest, around me! out of sight
Now float me of the vexing land abhorred,
Till in deep calms of space my soul may right
Her nature, shoot large sail on lengthening cord,
And rush exultant on the Infinite.

There's only one possible cure for being stuck in the muck of finite life, and that is to rush exultant on the infinite.

The Pilgrim
by Richard Wightman

I am my ancient self,
    Long paths I've trod,
The living light before,
    Behind, the rod:
And in the beam and blow
    The misty God.

I am my ancient self.
    My flesh is young,
But old, mysterious words
    Engage my tongue,
And weird, lost songs
    Old bards have sung.

I have not fared alone.
    In mount and dell
The one I fain would be
    Stands by me well,
And bids my man's heart list
    To the far bell.

Give me nor ease nor goal—
    Only the Way,
A bit of bread and sleep
    Where the white waters play,
The pines, the patient stars,
    And the new day.

Poems of Light — 36

The Little Tippler
by Emily Dickinson

I taste a liquor never brewed—
From Tankards scooped in Pearl—
Not all the Vats upon the Rhine
Yield such an Alcohol!

Inebriate of Air am I
And Debauchee of Dew—
Reeling thru endless summer days
From inns of Molten Blue.

When "Landlords" turn the drunken Bee
Out of the Foxglove's door—
When Butterflies renounce their "drams"
I shall but drink the more!

Till Seraphs swing their snowy Hats
And Saints to windows run—
To see the little Tippler
Leaning against the Sun.

A marvelous description of the way we are supposed to respond to the divine vitality of the inner life.

Today
by Thomas Carlyle

So here hath been dawning
    Another blue day:
Think, wilt thou let it
    Slip useless away?

Out of Eternity
    This new day is born;
Into Eternity
    At night will return.

Behold it afore time,
    No eye ever did:
So soon it forever
    From all eyes is hid.

Here hath been dawning
    Another blue day:
Think, wilt thou let it
    Slip useless away?

Creeds

The word "creed" derives from *credo,* or *I believe.* When we think of poetic creeds, generally it is Henley's powerful poem "Invictus" that comes to mind. But "Invictus" is written more in a tone of defiance than comprehension. It's basically the personality telling the soul, "Go ahead and stomp on me; I can take it." Instead of tapping the strength of spirit and learning to use it, he asserts his own personal strength.

The creeds, prayers, and statements of known facts gathered in the following few poems are much better creeds to live our lives by. If you need strength to overcome great odds, draw it from Whitman's "Grand is the Seen," instead of Henley's "Invictus." It's a cleaner, more noble and enriching kind of strength—the strength of spiritual purpose, not personal rebelliousness.

Ideally, a creed is meant to be a commitment to divine life and spiritual service, not just a statement of personal belief. "The Universal Prayer" by Alexander Pope comes closest to fulfilling this ideal.

Grand is the Seen
by Walt Whitman

Grand is the seen, the light, to me—
    grand are the sky and stars,
Grand is the earth,
    and grand are lasting time and space,
And grand their laws, so multiform,
    puzzling, evolutionary;
But grander far the unseen soul of me,
    comprehending, endowing all those,
Lighting the light, the sky and stars,
    delving the earth, sailing the sea,
(What were all those, indeed, without thee,
    unseen soul? of what amount without thee?)
More evolutionary, vast, puzzling, O my soul!
More multiform far—more lasting thou than they.

The Bohemian Hymn
by Ralph Waldo Emerson

In many forms we try
To utter God's infinity,
But the boundless hath no form,
And the Universal Friend
Doth as far transcend
An angel as a worm.

The great Idea baffles wit,
Language falters under it,
It leaves the learned in the lurch;
No art, nor power, nor toil can find
The measure of the eternal Mind,
Nor hymn, nor prayer, nor church.

To Althea, From Prison
by Richard Lovelace

When Love with unconfinèd wings
    Hovers within my gates,
And my divine Althea brings
    To whisper at the grates;
When I lie tangled in her hair
    And fetter'd to her eye,
The birds that wanton in the air
    Know no such liberty.

When flowing cups run swiftly round
    With no allaying Thames,
Our careless heads with roses bound,
    Our hearts with loyal flames;
When thirsty grief in wine we steep,
    When healths and draughts go free—
Fishes that tipple in the deep
    Know no such liberty.

When, like committed linnets, I
    With shriller throat shall sing
The sweetness, mercy, majesty,
    And glories of my King;
When I shall voice aloud how good
    He is, how great should be,
Enlargéd winds, that curl the flood,
    Know no such liberty.

Stone walls do not a prison make,
    Nor iron bars a cage;
Minds innocent and quiet take
    That for an hermitage.

Poems of Light — 42

If I have freedom in my love
    And in my soul am free,
Angels alone, that soar above,
    Enjoy such liberty.

> *Some of us become imprisoned in our own thoughts, attitudes—even our physical bodies. We can struggle against fate all we want, but the stone walls of our own limited world view will continue to entrap us—until we cultivate the larger view of the soul.*

A Creed
by John Masefield

I hold that when a person dies
    His soul returns again to earth;
Arrayed in some new flesh-disguise
    Another mother gives him birth.
With sturdier limbs and mightier brain
The old soul takes the roads again.

Such is my own belief and trust;
    This hand, this hand that holds the pen,
Has many hundred times been dust
    And turned, as dust, to dust again;
These eyes of mine have blinked and shone
In Thebes, in Troy, in Babylon.

All that I rightly think or do,
    Or make, or spoil, or bless, or blast,
Is curse or blessing justly due
    For sloth or effort in the past.
My life's a statement of the sum
Of vice indulged, or overcome.

I know that in my lives to be
    My sorry heart will ache and burn,
And worship unavailingly,
    The woman whom I used to spurn,
And shake to see another have
The love I spurned, the love she gave.

And I shall know, in angry words,
    In gibes, and mocks, and many a tear,

Poems of Light — 44

A carrion flock of homing-birds,
    The gibes and scorns I uttered here.
The brave word that I failed to speak
Will brand me dastard on the cheek.

And as I wander on the roads
    I shall be helped and healed and blessed;
Dear words shall cheer and be as goads
    To urge to heights before unguessed.
My road shall be the road I made;
All that I gave shall be repaid.

So shall I fight, so shall I tread,
    In this long war beneath the stars;
So shall a glory wreathe my head,
    So shall I faint and show the scars,
Until this case, this clogging mould,
Be smithied all to kingly gold.

The Universal Prayer
by Alexander Pope

Father of All! in every Age,
    In every Clime adored,
By Saint, by Savage, and by Sage,
    Jehovah, Jove, or Lord!

Thou Great First Cause, least understood:
    Who all my Sense confined
To know but this, that Thou art Good,
    And that myself am blind;

Yet gave me, in this dark Estate,
    To see the Good from Ill;
And binding Nature fast in Fate,
    Left free the Human Will.

What Conscience dictates to be done,
    Or warns me not to do,
This, teach me more than Hell to shun,
    That, more than Heaven pursue.

What Blessings thy free Bounty gives,
    Let me not cast away;
For God is paid when Man receives,
    T' enjoy is to obey.

Yet not to Earth's contracted Span
    Thy Goodness let me bound,
Or think Thee Lord alone of Man,
    When thousand Worlds are round:

Poems of Light — 46

Let not this weak, unknowing hand
    Presume thy bolts to throw,
And deal damnation round the land,
    On each I judge thy Foe.

If I am right, thy grace impart,
    Still in the right to stay;
If I am wrong, oh teach my heart
    To find that better way.

Save me alike from foolish Pride,
    Or impious Discontent,
At aught thy Wisdom has denied,
    Or aught thy Goodness lent.

Teach me to feel another's Woe,
    To hide the Fault I see;
That Mercy I to others show,
    That Mercy show to me.

Mean though I am, not wholly so,
    Since quickened by thy Breath;
Oh lead me wheresoe'er I go,
    Through this day's Life or Death.

This day, be Bread and Peace my Lot:
    All else beneath the Sun,
Thou know'st if best bestowed or not;
    And let Thy Will be done.

To thee, whose Temple is all Space,
    Whose Altar Earth, Sea, Skies,
One Chorus let all Being raise,
    All Nature's Incense rise!

Going To Church
by Emily Dickinson

Some keep Sunday going to church
    I keep it staying at home,
With a bobolink for a chorister,
    And an orchard for a throne.

Some keep Sabbath in surplice,
    I just wear my wings
And instead of tolling the bell for church,
    Our little sexton sings.

God preaches, a noted clergyman,
    And the sermon is never long,
So instead of going to heaven at last
    I'm going all along.

Pippa's Song
by Robert Browning

The year's at the spring,
And the day's at the morn;
Morning's at seven,
The hill-side's dew-pearl'd;
The lark's on the wing,
The snail's on the thorn;
God's in His heaven—
All's right with the world!

There may be hell to pay in our own lives, but who are we to impose our personal confusion and grief on the rest of the world? Instead, we should draw from God and Nature the light we need to restore balance and hope to our lives.

The Problem
by Ralph Waldo Emerson

I like a church; I like a cowl;
I love a prophet of the soul;
And on my heart monastic aisles
Fall like sweet strains or pensive smiles:
Yet not for all his faith can see,
Would I that cowled churchman be,
Why should the vest on him allure,
Which I could not on me endure?

Not from a vain or shallow thought
His awful Jove young Phidias brought;
Never from the lips of cunning fell
The thrilling Delphic oracle;
Out of the heart of Nature rolled
The burdens of the Bible old;
The litanies of nations came,
Like the volcano's tongue of flame,
Up from the burning core below—
The canticles of love and woe:
The hand that rounded Peter's dome,
And groined the aisles of Christian Rome,
Wrought in a sad sincerity;
Himself from God he could not free;
He builded better than he knew—
The conscious stone to beauty grew.

Know'st thou what wove yon woodbird's nest
Of leaves, and feathers from her breast?
Or how the fish outbuilt her shell,
Painting with morn each annual cell?

Or how the sacred pine-tree adds
To her old leaves new myriads?
Such and so grew these holy piles,
Whilst love and terror laid the tiles.
Earth proudly wears the Parthenon,
As the best gem upon her zone,
And Morning opes with haste her lids,
To gaze upon the Pyramids;
O'er England's abbeys bends the sky,
As on its friends, with kindred eye;
For, out of Thought's interior sphere,
These wonders rose to upper air;
And Nature gladly gave them place,
Adopted them into her race,
And granted them an equal date
With Andes and with Ararat.

These temples grew as grows the grass;
Art might obey but not surpass.
The passive master lent his hand,
To the vast soul that o'er him planned;
And the same power that reared the shrine
Bestrode the tribes that knelt within.
Ever the fiery Pentecost
Girds with one flame the countless host.
Trances the heart through chanting choirs,
And through the priest the mind inspires.
The word unto the prophet spoken
Was writ on tables yet unbroken;
The word by seer or sibyls told,
In groves of oak, or fanes of gold,
Still floats upon the morning wind,
Still whispers to the willing mind.
One accent of the Holy Ghost
The heedless world hath never lost.

I know what say the fathers wise—
The Book itself before me lies—
Old Chrysostom, best Augustine,
And he who blent both in his line,
The younger Golden Lips or mines,
Taylor, the Shakespeare of divines.
His words are music in my ear,
I see his cowlèd portrait dear;
And yet, for all his faith could see,
I would not the good bishop be.

Emerson's theme—that we must build the living presence of God on earth, rather than monuments to it—is one that churches have had a hard time understanding.

Transformation

    To continue Emerson's metaphor, the greatest cathedral of all is our own character, value system, and consciousness. Can God walk freely through the chambers of our mind and heart? Or must the soul sneak in steathily, under the cover of night, totally ignored except in furtive dreams?

    God comes to earth—Paradise is regained—as each of us transforms our self-expression from one of greed, selfishness, fear, and ignorance into one of light, joy, compassion, poise, and wisdom. It is not enough just to believe in God—we must build a proper temple in our own daily behavior and demonstrate for all the world to see that God does live. In us. In each of us.

    As Sara Teasdale discovers, this is the real magic of alchemy.

Alchemy
by Sara Teasdale

I lift my heart as spring lifts up
    A yellow daisy to the rain;
My heart will be a lovely cup
    Although it holds but pain.

For I shall learn from flower and leaf
    That color every drop they hold,
To change the lifeless wine of grief
    To living gold.

Actually, flowers are a perfect physical expression of the very divine qualities that heal our grief, our anxieties, and our depressions. They can help transform our emotional immaturity into living gold.

Merlin
by Carl Japikse

I. I am weary now
of tales told of me;
I come seeking vengeance,
I have been wronged,
my name ground beneath
the gilt-edge of sorcery,
my words of great armies
corrupted through chanting,
my spear-shafted mind
shackled by fools.
I, yes I, Myrddin,
Taliesen knew me,
Aneirin sang of me,
I sang of them.
No shame did we spill
drinking from mead-cups,
no loss did we suffer
retelling great battles,
no sin did we see
praising Urien,
describing the feasts
of renowned Mynyddawg.

II. In the time of Gododdin,
the courtyard of Beli,
the halls of Gwenddolau,
that kind-hearted lord,
I was a bard,
master of word-craft,
Myrddin the ode-singer.
I witnessed brave feats,

brought great men cheer
on the eve of the battle;
the armor and shields
lay waiting in darkness.

III. I lived on sweet wine,
died, mad, in the woods,
after the striving
on the fields of Arfderydd
made widows of wives,
vigil for Myrddin.
Fire-brand Aeron,
lion-lord Cynon,
wept at my graveside
then sped to their havoc.

IV. Centuries later,
the warriors forgotten,
their mead halls in ruin,
their valor forsaken,
their deeds trampled over,
my defenders defeated,
my name was exhumed,
enchanted by Arthur,
not as a bard
but green-veiled magician,
my similes tarnished
to vain incantations,
my rhetoric ravaged
for potions and powders,
hyperbole slaughtered
on fields of dark spells,
my pure gold transmuted
by base-hearted wizards
into alchemic ingots of iron.

V. There I lay, trapped,
centuries and centuries,
in penny romances,
trouble-filled cauldrons.
The stench, the ardor
sweated my brow.
No salvation
in staving off rabble;
when the tale is told,
long was my fate.

VI. The fires of the sorcerers,
unstemmed by endurance;
I held steadfast,
no firmer in trial
than stubborn in battle.
Twelve hundred, red armored,
demonic and fierce;
twelve hundred, hungry,
consumed me like fever.
My words fell apart,
delivered to dust.

VII. The fires of the sorcerers,
dead in the distance,
twelve hundred, red armored,
writhe on the field.
My strong heart sustains me,
my words are the victors;
now to the mead halls
I ride a white stallion.

VIII. I am Myrddin of words
not Merlin of magic;
yet with sorrow

not sought for,
advantage is nurtured.
From bard into magus,
now magus to bard,
I speak a new language,
I sing a new song.
No longer the warriors,
savage in battle;
no longer pale mead
their portion, their poison;
no longer the monarchs
standing in court.
No longer mad Merlin,
stark in the forest;
I stand on the hilltop
stalwart, courageous;
I stand on the hilltop
to throw down my gage.
From gold into iron
to return into gold,
from gold into iron
to improve upon gold.

Or, "From light to obscurity, to cast out the darkness." The light we glimpse often becomes the enchantment that imprisons us long years, until we realize the difference between divine reality— and our opinion of it.

I Ponder'd in Silence
by Walt Whitman

As I ponder'd in silence,
Returning upon my poems, considering, lingering long,
A Phantom arose before me with distrustful aspect,
Terrible in beauty, age, and power,
The genius of poets of old lands,
As to me directing like flames its eyes,
With finger pointing to many immortal songs,
And menacing voice, *What singest thou?* it said,
Know'st thou not there is but one theme for ever-enduring bards?
And that is the theme of War, the fortune of battles,
The making of perfect soldiers.
Be it so, then I answer'd,
I too haughty Shade also sing war, and a longer and greater
　one than any,
Waged in my book with varying fortune, with flight,
　advance, and retreat, victory deferr'd and wavering,
(Yet methinks certain, or as good as certain, at the last),
　the field the world,
For life and death, for the Body and for the eternal Soul,
Lo, I too am come, chanting the chant of battles,
I above all promote brave soldiers.

A Prayer in Spring
by Robert Frost

Oh, give us pleasure in the flowers today;
And give us not to think so far away
As the uncertain harvest; keep us here
All simply in the springing of the year.

Oh, give us pleasure in the orchard white,
Like nothing else by day, like ghosts by night;
And make us happy in the happy bees,
The swarm dilating round the perfect trees.

And make us happy in the darting bird
That suddenly above the bees is heard,
The meteor that thrusts in with needle bill,
And off a blossom in mid-air stands still.

For this is love and nothing else is love,
The which it is reserved for God above
To sanctify to what far ends He will,
But which it only needs that we fulfill.

A Phantom of Delight
by William Wordsworth

She was a Phantom of delight
When first she gleamed upon my sight;
A lovely Apparition, sent
To be a moment's ornament;
Her eyes as stars of Twilight fair;
Like Twilight's, too, her dusky hair;
But all things else about her drawn
From May-time and the cheerful Dawn;
A dancing Shape, an Image gay,
To haunt, to startle, and way-lay.

I saw her upon nearer view,
A Spirit, yet a Woman too!
Her household motions light and free,
And steps of virgin-liberty;
A countenance in which did meet
Sweet records, promises as sweet;
A Creature not too bright or good
For human nature's daily food;
For transient sorrows, simple wiles,
Praise, blame, love, kisses, tears, and smiles.

And now I see with eye serene
The very pulse of the machine;
A Being breathing thoughtful breath,
A Traveller between life and death;
The reason firm, the temperate will,
Endurance, foresight, strength, and skill;

A perfect Woman, nobly planned,
To warn, to comfort, and command;
And yet a Spirit still, and bright
With something of angelic light.

> *We are all spiritual beings occupying our dense physical bodies, man or woman, yet hardly any of us takes the time or trouble to share this angelic presence with others, as did Wordsworth's wife. Each of us should so live our lives that at the end, no one will quite be able to decide if we were human—or divine.*

The Symbolic and the Real
by Carl Japikse

I am the Symbolic and the Real,
A fragment of heaven come to earth;
The image of the Great One's seal,
I am the Symbolic and the Real.

Through tests and triumphs I reveal
Humanity's destiny and worth;
I am the Symbolic and the Real,
A fragment of heaven come to earth.

Thought
by Christopher Pease Cranch

Thought is deeper than all speech,
    Feeling deeper than all thought,
Souls to souls can never teach
    What unto themselves was taught.

We are spirits clad in veils;
    Man by man was never seen;
All our deep communing fails
    To remove the shadowy screen.

Heart to heart was never known;
    Mind with mind did never meet;
We are columns left alone
    Of a temple once complete.

Like the stars that gem the sky,
    Far apart, though seeming near,
In our light we scattered lie;
    All is thus but starlight here.

What is social company
    But a babbling summer stream?
What our wise philosophy
    But the glancing of a dream?

Only when the sun of love
    Melts the scattered stars of thought,
Only when we live above
    What the dim-eyed world hath taught,

Poems of Light — 64

Only when our souls are fed
    By the fount which gave them birth,
And by inspiration led
    Which they never drew from earth,

We, like parted drops of rain,
    Swelling till they meet and run,
Shall be all absorbed again,
    Melting, flowing into one.

A Sonnet
by John Masefield

O little self, within whose smallness lies
All that a man was, and is, and will become,
Atom unseen that comprehends the skies
And tells the tracks by which the planets roam.
That, without moving, knows the joy of wings,
The tiger's strength, the eagle's secrecy,
And in the hovel can consort with kings,
Or clothe a god with his own mystery.
O, with what darkness do we cloak thy light,
What dusty folly gather thee for food,
Thou who alone art knowledge and delight,
The heavenly bread, the beautiful, the good.
O living self, O god, O morning star,
Give us thy light, forgive us what we are.

Brahma
by Ralph Waldo Emerson

If the red slayer think he slays,
    Or if the slain think he is slain,
They know not well the subtle ways
    I keep, and pass, and turn again.

Far or forgot to me is near;
    Shadow and sunlight are the same;
The vanished gods to me appear;
    And one to me are shame and fame.

They reckon ill who leave me out;
    When me they fly, I am the wings;
I am the doubter and the doubt,
    And I the hymn the Brahmin sings.

The strong gods pine for my abode,
    And pine in vain the sacred Seven;
But thou, meek lover of the good!
    Find me, and turn thy back on heaven.

The admonition to turn our backs on heaven does not, of course, mean that we ignore the light of divine life. On the contrary, once we have harnessed the duality of light and darkness, we are meant to involve ourselves in service on earth (by turning our back to heaven) and share the light we have made ours with others.

The Trial by Existence
by Robert Frost

Even the bravest that are slain
    Shall not dissemble their surprise
On waking to find valor reign,
    Even as on earth, in paradise;
And where they sought without the sword
    Wide fields of asphodel fore'er,
To find that the utmost reward
    Of daring should be still to dare.

The light of heaven falls whole and white
    And is not shattered into dyes,
The light forever is morning light;
    The hills are verdured pasturewise.
The angel hosts with freshness go,
    And seek with laughter what to brave—
And binding all is the hushed snow
    Of the far-distant breaking wave.

And from a cliff top is proclaimed
    The gathering of the souls for birth,
The trial by existence is named.
    The obscuration upon earth.
And the slant spirits trooping by
    In streams and cross- and counter-streams
Can but give ear to that sweet cry
    For its suggestion of what dreams!

And the more loitering are turned
    To view once more the sacrifice
Of those who for some good discerned
    Will gladly give up paradise.

And a white shimmering concourse rolls
    Toward the throne to witness there
The speeding of devoted souls
    Which God makes his especial care.

And none are taken but who will,
    Having first heard the life read out
That opens earthward, good and ill,
    Beyond the shadow of a doubt;
And very beautifully, God limns,
    And tenderly, life's little dream,
But naught extenuates or dims,
    Setting the thing that is supreme.

Nor is there wanting in the press
    Some spirit to stand simply forth,
Heroic in its nakedness,
    Against the uttermost of earth.
The tale of earth's unhonored things
    Sounds nobler there than 'neath the sun;
And the mind whirls and the heart sings,
    And a shout greets the daring one.

But always God speaks at the end:
    "One thought in agony of strife
The bravest would have by for friend,
    The memory that he chose the life;
But the pure fate to which you go
    Admits no memory of choice,
Or the woe were not earthy woe
    To which you give the assenting voice."

And so the choice must be again,
    But the last choice is still the same;

And the awe passes wonder then,
    And a hush falls for all acclaim.
And God has taken a flower of gold
    And broken it, and used therefrom
The mystic link to bind and hold
    Spirit to matter till death come.

'Tis of the essence of life here,
    Though we choose greatly, still to lack
The lasting memory at all clear,
    That life has for us on the wrack
Nothing but what we somehow chose;
    Thus are we wholly stripped of pride
In the pain that has but one close,
    Bearing it crushed and mystified.

The Overheart
by John Greenleaf Whittier

Above, below, in the sky and sod
    In leaf and spar, in star and man,
    Well might the wise Athenian scan
The geometric signs of God,
    The measured order of his plan.

And India's mystics sang aright
    Of the One Life pervading all—
    One Being's tidal rise and fall
In soul and form, in sound and sight—
    Eternal outflow and recall.

God is: and man in guilt and fear
    This central fact of Nature owns;
    Kneels, trembling, by his altar-stones,
And darkly dreams the ghastly smear.

Guilt shapes by Terror: deep within
    The human heart the secret lies
    Of all the hideous deities;
And, painted on a ground of sin,
    The fabled gods of torment rise!

And what is He?—The ripe grain nods,
    The sweet dews fall, the flowers blow;
    But darker signs his presence show:
The earthquake and the storm are God's
    And good and evil interflow.

O hearts of love! O souls that turn
    Like sunflowers to the pure and best!
    To you the truth is manifest:
For they the mind of Christ discern
    Who lean like John upon his breast!

In him of whom the Sybil told
    For whom the prophet's heart was toned,
    Whose need the sage and magian owned,
The loving heart of God behold,
    The hope for which the ages groaned!

Fade, pomp of dreadful imagery
    Wherewith mankind have deified
    Their hate, and selfishness, and pride!
Let the sacred dreamer wake to see
    The Christ of Nazareth at his side!

What doth that holy Guide require?
    No rite of pain, nor gift of blood,
    But man a kindly brotherhood,
Looking, where duty is desire,
    To him, the beautiful and good.

Gone be the faithlessness of fear,
    And let the pitying heaven's sweet rain
    Wash out the altar's bloody stain;
The law of Hatred disappear,
    The law of Love alone remain.

How fall the idols false and grim!
    And, Lo! the hideous wreck above
    The emblems of the Lamb and Dove!
Man turns from God, not God from him,
    And guilt, in suffering, whispers Love!

Poems of Light — 72

The world sits at the feet of Christ,
    Unknowing, blind and unconsoled;
    It yet shall touch his garment's fold,
And feel the heavenly Alchemist
    Transform its very dust to gold.

The theme befitting angel tongues
    Beyond a mortal's scope has grown.
    O heart of mine, with reverence own
The fulness which to it belongs,
    And trust the unknown for the known.

Revelation
by Robert Frost

We make ourselves a place apart
    Behind light words that tease and flout,
But oh, the agitated heart
    Till someone really finds us out.

'Tis pity if the case require
    (Or as we say) that in the end
We speak the literal to inspire
    The understanding of a friend.

But so with all, from babes that play
    At hide-and-seek to God afar,
So all who hide too well away
    Must speak and tell us where they are.

It is our own effort to examine the hidden secrets of our heart that leads to divine revelation. It only makes sense: God is able to speak to us only when we are able to listen clearly, honestly, and responsively to our own inner patterns of truth and wisdom.

Divine Life and Laws

A lot of people excuse themselves from honest efforts at spiritual growth by stating: "How can I know what God wants for me?" Since this seems like an unanswerable question, they make no effort to answer it.

If we lead a self-examined, reflective life, however, the question becomes answerable. As we become aware of the intelligent patterns that have governed our own humble life, we gradually become aware that all of life is pervaded by this self-same intelligence. The world is an orderly sphere, governed by divine laws that we can come to know and count on.

The challenge, for each of us, is to take what we know about divine life and translate it into our own daily conduct. What good does it serve, after all, to know that "as you sow, so shall you reap," unless you begin acting in generous, helpful, and considerate ways? What good does it serve to know that God is all-forgiving if we poison our lives by refusing to forgive others for their misdeeds?

The more we know about God's life and ways, the greater our opportunity to mend our ways. Although the ancient maxim promises us "as above, so below," this only becomes a true statement for us as we begin acting and responding to life with divine inspiration.

Light Shining Out of Darkness
by William Cowper

God moves in a mysterious way
    His wonders to perform;
He plants his footsteps in the sea,
    And rides upon the storm.

Deep in unfathomable mines
    Of never-failing skill
He treasures up his bright designs,
    And works his sovereign will.

Ye fearful saints, fresh courage take,
    The clouds ye so much dread
Are big with mercy, and shall break
    In blessings on your head.

Judge not the Lord by feeble sense,
    But trust him for his grace:
Behind a frowning providence
    He hides a smiling face.

His purposes will ripen fast,
    Unfolding every hour;
The bud may have a bitter taste
    But sweet will be the flower.

Blind unbelief is sure to err,
    And scan his work in vain;
God is his own interpreter
    And he will make it plain.

Theophany
by Evelyn Underhill

Deep cradled in the fringed mow to lie
And feel the rhythmic flux of life sweep by,
This is to know the easy heaven that waits
Before our timidly-embattled gates:
To show the exultant leap and thrust of things
Outward toward perfection, in the heart
Of every bud to see the folded wings,
Discern the patient whole in every part.

Life's Reverberation
by Emily Dickinson

The farthest Thunder that I heard
Was nearer than the Sky
And rumbles still, though torrid Noons
Have lain their missiles by.

The Lightning that preceded it
Struck no one but myself,
But I would not exchange the Bolt
For all the rest of Life.

Indebtedness to Oxygen
The Happy may repay,
But not the obligation
To Electricity.

It founds the Homes and decks the Days
And every clamor bright
Is but the gleam concomitant
Of that waylaying Light.

The Thought is quiet as a Flake—
A Crash without a Sound,
How Life's reverberation
Its Explanation found.

Shoestring
by Carl Japikse

In morning class I learned
How galaxies are made,
Which helps me with my task
Of building molecules.

You see, I can't afford
Galactic two by eights;
With limited funds, you
Do as much as you can.

The Informing Spirit
by Ralph Waldo Emerson

There is no great and no small
To the Soul that maketh all:
And where it cometh, all things are;
And it cometh everywhere.

I am owner of the sphere,
Of the seven stars and the solar year,
Of Caesar's hand, and Plato's brain,
Of Lord Christ's heart, and Shakespeare's strain.

Song of the Universal
by Walt Whitman

1. Come said the Muse,
Sing me a song no poet yet has chanted,
Sing me the universal.

In this broad earth of ours,
Amid the measureless grossness and the slag,
Enclosed and safe within its central heart,
Nestles the seed perfection.

By every life a share or more or less,
None born but it is born, conceal'd or unconceal'd
    the seed is waiting.

2. Lo! keen-eyed towering science,
As from tall peaks the modern overlooking,
Successive absolute fiats issuing.

Yet again, lo! the soul, above all science,
For it has history gather'd like husks around the globe,
For it the entire star-myriads roll through the sky.

In spiral routes by long detours,
(As a much-tacking ship upon the sea),
For it the partial to the permanent flowing,
For it the real to the ideal tends.

For it is the mystic evolution,
Not the right only justified, what we call evil also justified.

Forth from their masks, no matter what,

From the huge festering trunk, from craft and guile and
    tears,
Health to emerge and joy, joy universal.

Out of the bulk, the morbid and the shallow,
Out of the bad majority, the varied countless frauds of
    men and states,
Electric, antiseptic yet, cleaving, suffusing all,
Only the good is universal.

3. Over the mountain-growths disease and sorrow,
An uncaught bird is ever hovering, hovering,
High in the purer, happier air.

From imperfection's murkiest cloud,
Darts always forth one ray of perfect light,
One flash of heaven's glory.

To fashion's, custom's discord,
To the mad Babel-din, the deafening orgies,
Soothing each lull a strain is heard, just heard,
From some far shore the final chorus sounding.

O the blest eyes, the happy hearts,
That see, that know the guiding thread so fine,
Along the mighty labyrinth.

4. And thou America,
For the scheme's culmination, its thought and its reality,
For these (and not thyself) thou hast arrived.

Thou too surroundest all,
Embracing carrying welcoming all, thou too by pathways
    broad and new,
To the ideal tendest.

Poems of Light — 82

The measur'd faiths of other lands, the grandeurs of the
    past,
Are not for thee, but grandeurs of thine own,
Deific faiths and amplitudes, absorbing, comprehending
    all,
All eligible to all.

All, all for immortality,
Love like the light silently wrapping all,
Nature's amelioration blessing all,
The blossoms, fruits of ages, orchards divine and certain,
Forms, objects, growths, humanities, to spiritual images
    ripening.

Give me O God to sing that thought,
Give me, give him or her I love this quenchless faith
In Thy ensemble, whatever else withheld withhold not
    from us,
Belief in plan of Thee enclosed in Time and Space,
Health, peace, salvation universal.

Is it a dream?
Nay but the lack of it the dream,
And failing it life's lore and wealth a dream,
And all the world a dream.

An Essay on Man
by Alexander Pope

EPISTLE ONE, PART VII

Far as Creation's ample range extends,
The scale of sensual, mental powers ascends:
Mark how it mounts, to Man's imperial race,
From the green myriads in the peopled grass:
What modes of sight betwixt each wide extreme,
The mole's dim curtain, and the lynx's beam:
Of smell, the headlong lioness between,
And hound sagacious on the tainted green:
O hearing, from the life that fills the flood,
To that which warbles through the vernal wood:
The spider's touch, how exquisitely fine!
Feels at each thread, and lives along the line:
In the nice bee, what sense so subtly true
From pois'nous herbs extracts the healing dew?
How Instinct varies in the grov'lling swine,
Compared, half-reas'ning elephant, with thine!
'Twixt that, and Reason, what a nice barrier,
For ever sep'rate, yet for ever near!
Remembrance and Reflection how allied!
What thin partitions Sense from Thought divide:
And Middle natures, how they long to join,
Yet never pass th' insuperable line!
Without this just gradation, could they be
Subjected, these to those, or all to thee?
The powers of all subdued by thee alone,
Is not thy Reason all these powers in one?

VIII. See, through this air, this ocean, and this earth,
All matter quick, and bursting into birth.
Above, how high, progressive life may go!
Around, how wide! how deep extend below!
Vast chain of Being! which from God began,
Natures ethereal, human, angel, man,
Beast, bird, fish, insect, what no eye can see,
What no glass can reach; from Infinite to thee,
From thee to Nothing. On superior powers
Were we to press, inferior might on ours:
Or in the full creation leave a void,
Where, one step broken, the great scale's destroyed:
From Nature's chain whatever link you strike,
Tenth or ten thousandth, breaks the chain alike.
   And, if each system in gradation roll
Alike essential to th' amazing Whole,
The least confusion but in one, not all
That system only, but the Whole must fall.
Let Earth unbalanced from her orbit fly,
Planets and Suns run lawless through the sky;
Let ruling Angels from their spheres be hurled,
Being on Being wrecked, and world on world;
Heaven's whole foundations to their centre nod,
And Nature trembles to the throne of God:
All this dread ORDER break—for whom? for thee?
Vile worm! Oh Madness! Pride! Impiety!

   IX. What if the foot, ordained the dust to tread,
Or hand, to toil, aspired to be the head?
What if the head, the eye, or ear repined
To serve mere engines to the ruling Mind?
Just as absurd for any part to claim
To be another, in this gen'ral frame:
Just as absurd, to mourn the tasks or pains,
The great directing MIND OF ALL ordains.

All are but parts of one stupendous whole,
Whose body Nature is, and God the soul;
That, changed through all, and yet in all the same;
Great in the earth, as in th' ethereal frame;
Warms in the sun, refreshes in the breeze,
Glows in the stars, and blossoms in the trees,
Lives through all life, extends through all extent,
Spreads undivided, operates unspent;
Breathes in our soul, informs our mortal part,
As full, as perfect, in a hair as heart:
As full, as perfect, in vile Man that mourns,
As the rapt Seraph that adores and burns;
To him no high, no low, no great, no small;
He fills, he bounds, connects, and equals all.

X. Cease then, nor ORDER Imperfection name:
Our proper bliss depends on what we blame.
Know thy own point: This kind, this due degree
Of blindness, weakness, Heaven bestows on thee.
Submit. In this, or any other sphere,
Secure to be as blest as thou canst bear:
Safe in the hand of one disposing Power,
Or in the natal, or the mortal hour.
All Nature is but Art, unknown to thee;
All Chance, Direction, which thou canst not see;
All Discord, Harmony not understood;
All partial Evil, universal Good:
And, spite of Pride, in erring Reason's spite,
One truth is clear, WHATEVER IS, IS RIGHT.

Epistle Two, Part I

    Know then thyself, presume not God to scan;
The proper study of Mankind is Man.
Placed on this isthmus of a middle state,
A Being darkly wise, and rudely great:
With too much knowledge for the Skeptic side,
With too much weakness for the Stoic's pride,
He hangs between; in doubt to act, or rest;
In doubt to deem himself a God, or Beast;
In doubt his Mind or Body to prefer;
Born but to die, and reas'ning but to err;
Alike in ignorance, his reason such,
Whether he thinks too little, or too much:
Chaos of Thought and Passion, all confused;
Still by himself abused, or disabused;
Created half to rise, and half to fall;
Great lord of all things, yet a prey to all;
Sole judge of Truth, in endless Error hurled:
The glory, jest, and riddle of the world!
    Go, wondrous creature! mount where Science guides;
Go, measure earth, weigh air, and state the tides;
Instruct the planets in what orbs to run,
Correct old Time, and regulate the Sun;
Go, soar with Plato to th' empyreal sphere,
To the first good, first perfect, and first fair;
Or tread the mazy round his follow'rs trod,
And quitting sense call imitating God;
As Eastern priests in giddy circles run,
And turn their heads to imitate the Sun.
Go, teach Eternal Wisdom how to rule—
Then drop into thyself, and be a fool!

EPISTLE FOUR, PART VII

    Know then this truth (enough for Man to know)
"Virtue alone is Happiness below."
The only point where human bliss stands still,
And tastes the good without the fall to ill;
Where only Merit constant pay receives,
Is blest in what it takes, and what it gives;
The joy unequalled, if its end it gain,
And if it lose, attended with no pain:
Without satiety, though e'er so blessed,
And but more relished as the more distressed:
The broadest mirth unfeeling Folly wears,
Less pleasing far than Virtue's very tears:
Good, from each object, from each piece acquired,
For ever exercised, yet never tired!
Never elated, while one man's oppressed;
Never dejected, while another's blessed;
And where no wants, no wishes can remain,
Since but to wish more Virtue, is to gain.
    See the sole bliss Heaven could on all bestow!
Which who but feels can taste, but thinks can know:
Yet poor with fortune, and with learning blind,
The bad must pass; the good, untaught, will find;
Slave to no sect, who takes no private road,
But looks through Nature up to Nature's God;
Pursues that Chain which links the immense design,
Joins heaven and earth, immortal and divine;
Sees, that no Being any bliss can know,
But touches some above, and some below;
Learns, from this union of the rising Whole,
The first, last purpose of the human soul;
And knows, where Faith, Law, Morals, all began,
All end, in LOVE OF GOD, and LOVE OF MAN.

For him alone, Hope leads from goal to goal,
And opens still, and opens on his soul;
'Till lengthened on to Faith, and unconfined,
It pours the bliss that fills up all the mind.
He sees, why Nature plants in Man alone
Hope of known bliss, and Faith in bliss unknown;
(Nature, whose dictates to no other kind
Are given in vain, but what they seek they find)
Wise is her present; she connects in this
His greatest Virtue with his greatest Bliss;
At once his own bright prospect to be blest,
And strongest motive to assist the rest.
   Self-love thus pushed to social, to divine,
Gives thee to make thy neighbour's blessing thine.
Is this too little for thy boundless heart?
Extend it, let thy enemies have part:
Grasp the whole worlds of Reason, Life, and Sense,
In one close system of Benevolence:
Happier as kinder, in whate'er degree,
And height of Bliss but height of Charity.
   God loves from Whole to Parts: but human soul
Must rise from Individual to Whole.
Self-love but serves the virtuous mind to wake,
As the small pebble stirs the peaceful lake;
The centre moved, a circle straight succeeds,
Another still, and still another spreads;
Friend, parent, neighbour, first it will embrace;
His country next; and next all human race;
Wide and more wide, th' o'erflowings of the mind
Take every creature in, of every kind;
Earth smiles around, with boundless bounty blest,
And Heaven beholds its image in his breast.

The Calming Thought of All
by Walt Whitman

That coursing on, whate'er men's speculations,
Amid the changing schools, theologies, philosophies,
Amid the bawling presentations new and old,
The round earth's silent vital laws, facts, modes continue.

> *Not understanding divine life and law, we vastly overrate our own daily activities—both the triumphs and the tragedies. We become absorbed in the sponge of triviality of daily living. The only way to counter this is to cultivate "The Big Picture"—a sense of the wholeness and completeness of God's Creation.*

Inspiration

The chief spiritual duty of mankind is something far greater than just accepting God and believing in Him; we are called to become the "missing link" between heaven and earth. This means becoming a conduit by which some facet of the light of divine life can illumine the dark shadows of earth each and every day that we live.

The process of tapping divine light is called inspiration. But it is never enough just to be filled with light; we must then find a useful and helpful way of expressing this light for the benefit of others around us—indeed, all of life. The poets show us how this process works when they tap inspiration and restate it in a light-filled poem, but we do not have to be poets in order to participate in this process. We can be ordinary human beings—because ordinary human beings have the opportunity to—

Tap the inspiration of divine joy and express it to those who sorrow.

Tap the inspiration of divine goodwill and express it through forgiveness of those who have hurt us.

Tap the inspiration of divine dedication and express it through the quality of work we perform.

Tap the inspiration of divine wisdom and radiate it through our understanding of the complexities of life.

Tap the inspiration of divine peace and become an agent of it, by acting as a peacemaker in our own life.

To do this, we must learn to tap the ideal forces of divine life—what Keats names essences, Whitman calls eidólons, Elizabeth Barrett Browning labels antitypes, and what I would refer to as divine archetypes. These are the perfect patterns of divine life from which all inspiration is drawn.

Preface to Endymion
by John Keats

A thing of beauty is a joy for ever:
Its loveliness increases; it will never
Pass into nothingness; but still will keep
A bower quiet for us, and a sleep
Full of sweet dreams, and health, and quiet breathing.
Therefore, on every morrow, are we wreathing
A flowery band to bind us to the earth,
Spite of despondence, of the inhuman dearth
Of noble natures, of the gloomy days,
Of the unhealthy and o'er-darkened ways
Made for our searching: yes, in spite of all,
Some shape of beauty moves away the pall
From our dark spirits. Such the sun, the moon,
Trees old and young, sprouting a shady boon
For simple sheep; and such as daffodils
With the green world they live in; and clear rills
That for themselves a cooling covert make
'Gainst the hot season; the mid forest brake,
Rich with a sprinkling of fair musk-rose blooms:
And such too is the grandeur of the dooms
We have imagined for the mighty dead;
All lovely tales that we have heard or read:
An endless fountain of immortal drink,
Pouring unto us from the heaven's brink.

Nor do we merely feel these essences
For one short hour; no, even as the trees
That whisper round a temple become soon
Dear as the temple's self, so does the moon,

Poems of Light — 92

The passion poesy, glories infinite,
Haunt us till they become a cheering light
Unto our souls, and bound to us so fast,
That, whether there be shine, or gloom o'ercast,
They alway must be with us, or we die.

> *The "endless fountain of immortal drink" which contains these essences can also be thought of as the words issuing forth from the mouth of God, as described by the Christ in response to the first temptation. Beauty is one of the most accessible of these essences; we are meant to drink from its wide and varied presence daily, and thus commune with God. When we fail to do so, and huddle in our "dark spirits," we give in to the temptation to accept crudeness and vulgarity as part of our life.*

Genius
by Edward Lucas White

He cried aloud to God: "The men below
Are happy, for I see them come and go,
Parents and mates and friends, paired, clothed with love;
They heed not, see not, need me not above—
I am alone here. Grant me love and peace,
Or if not them, grant me at least release."

God answered him: "I set you here on high
Upon my beacon tower, you know not why,
Your soul-torch by the cruel gale is blown,
As desperate as our aching heart is lone.
You may not guess but that it shines in vain,
Yet, till it is burned out, you must remain."

Tending the light of genius can be a lonely vigil, unappreciated, misunderstood. But just as God's love and light never shines in vain, true genius never betrays its origin.

Eidólons
by Walt Whitman

    I met a seer,
Passing the hues and objects of the world,
The fields of art and learning, pleasure, sense,
    To glean eidólons.

    Put in thy chants said he,
No more the puzzling hour nor day, nor segments,
    parts, put in,
Put first before the rest as light for all and entrance-song
    of all,
    That of eidólons.

    Ever the dim beginning,
Ever the growth, the rounding of the circle,
Ever the summit and the merge at last,
    (to surely start again!)
    Eidólons! Eidólons!

    Ever the mutable,
Ever materials, changing, crumbling, re-cohering,
Ever the ateliers, the factories divine,
    Issuing eidólons.

    Lo, I or you,
Or woman, man, or state, known or unknown,
We seeming solid wealth, strength, beauty build,
    But really build eidólons.

The ostent evanescent,
The substances of an artist's mood or savan's studies long,
Or warrior's, martyr's, hero's toils,
    To fashion his eidólon.

Of every human life,
(The units gather'd, posted, not a thought, emotion,
    deed, left out),
The whole or large or small summ'd, added up,
    In its eidólon.

The old, old urge,
Based on the ancient pinnacles, lo, newer, higher
    pinnacles,
From science and the modern still impell'd,
    The old, old urge, eidólons.

The present now and here,
America's busy, teeming, intricate whirl,
Of aggregate and segregate for only thence releasing,
    Today's eidólons.

These with the past,
Of vanish'd lands, of all the reigns of kings across the sea,
Old conquerors, old campaigns, old sailor's voyages,
    Joining eidólons.

Densities, growth, façades,
Strata of mountains, soils, rocks, giant trees,
Far-born, far-dying, living long, to leave,
    Eidólons everlasting.

Exaltè, rapt, ecstatic,
The visible but their womb of birth,
Of orbic tendencies to shape and shape and shape,
    The mighty earth-eidólon.

    All space, all time,
(The stars, the terrible perturbations of the suns,
Swelling, collapsing, ending, serving their longer,
    shorter use),
    filled with eidólons only.

    The noiseless myriads,
The infinite oceans where the rivers empty,
The separate countless free identities, like eyesight,
    The true realities, eidólons.

    Not this the world,
Not these the universes, they the universes,
Purport and end, ever the permanent life of life,
    Eidólons, eidólons,

    Beyond thy lectures learn'd professor,
Beyond thy telescope or spectroscope observer keen,
    beyond all mathematics,
Beyond the doctor's surgery, anatomy, beyond the
    chemist with his chemistry,
    The entities of entities, eidólons.

    Unfix'd yet fix'd,
Ever shall be, ever have been and are,
Sweeping the present to the infinite future,
    Eidólons, eidólons, eidólons.

The prophet and the bard,
Shall yet maintain themselves, in higher stages yet,
Shall mediate to the Modern, to Democracy,
    interpret yet to them,
    God and eidólons.

And thee my soul,
Joys, ceaseless exercises, exaltations,
Thy yearning amply fed at last, prepared to meet,
    Thy mates, eidólons.

Thy body permanent,
The body lurking there within thy body,
The only purport of the form thou art, the real I myself,
    An image, an eidólon.

Thy very songs not in thy songs,
No special strains to sing, none for itself,
But from the whole resulting, rising at last and floating,
    A round full-orb'd eidólon.

> *"Eidólon" could roughly be translated as "the heart of an idea," the abstract inner essence or pattern from which all true inspiration arises. These are the patterns and plans of the mind of God. The spiritual person learns to tap these patterns and express them in all that he or she does.*

Pound for Pound
by Emily Dickinson

The Brain is wider than the Sky,
For put them side by side—
The one the other will contain
With ease—and You—beside.

The Brain is deeper than the sea,
For hold them Blue to Blue,
The one the other will absorb,
As Sponges—Buckets—do.

The Brain is just the weight of God,
For heft them Pound for Pound,
And they will differ—if they do—
As Syllable from Sound.

For That I Came
by Gerard Manley Hopkins

As kingfishers catch fire, dragonflies draw flame;
As tumbled over rim in roundy wells
Stones ring; like each tucked string tells,
    each hung bell's
Bow swung finds tongue to fling out broad its name;
Each mortal thing does one thing and the same:
Deals out that being indoors each one dwells;
Selves—goes itself; *myself* it speaks and spells,
Crying *What I do is me: for that I came.*

I say more: the just man justices;
Keeps grace: that keeps all his goings graces;
Acts in God's eye what in God's eye he is—
Christ—for Christ plays in ten thousand places,
Lovely in limbs, and lovely in eyes not his
To the Father through the features of men's faces.

The Genius of the Place
by Alexander Pope

(An excerpt from the epistle to the Earl of Burlington)

     Oft have you hinted to your Brother Peer,
A certain Truth, which many buy too dear:
Something there is more needful than Expense,
And something previous ev'n to Taste—'Tis *Sense:*
Good Sense, which only is the Gift of Heav'n,
And tho' no science, fairly worth the Seven:
A Light, which in yourself you must perceive;
Jones and Le Nôtre have it not to give.
     To build, to plant, whatever you intend,
To rear the column, or the arch to bend,
To swell the terrace, or to sink the grot;
In all, let *Nature* never be forgot.
But treat the goddess like a modest fair,
Nor overdress, nor leave her wholly bare;
Let not each beauty everywhere be spied,
Where half the skill is decently to hide.
He gains all points, who pleasingly confounds,
Surprises, varies, and conceals the bounds.
     Consult the *Genius of the Place* in all;
That tells the Waters or to rise, or fall;
Or helps th' ambitious Hill the Heav'ns to scale,
Or scoops in circling Theatres the Vale;
Calls in the Country, catches opening Glades,
Joins willing Woods, and varies Shades from Shades;
Now breaks, or now directs, th' intending Lines;
Paints as you plant, and, as you work, *Designs.*
     Still follow *Sense,* of ev'ry Art the Soul,
Parts answering Parts shall slide into a Whole,

Spontaneous Beauties all around advance,
Start ev'n from *Difficulty*, strike from *Chance;*
Nature shall join you; *Time* shall make it grow
A Work to wonder at—perhaps a Stowe.*

* Stowe was one of the most famous gardens of Pope's time—a model he held up as an example of perfection.

> *Pope is outlining rules for landscaping, yet they apply equally well to any form of inspiration. The unique quality of this passage is its profound insight into man's potential to interact artistically with nature as a living force or being. He was obviously aware of the angelic forces that supervise all aspects of nature—and knew that these forces would join with human effort, if enlightened.*

Inspiration
by Wilfrid Wilson Gibson

On the outermost far-flung ridge of ice and snow
That over pits of sunset fire hangs sheer
My naked spirit poises, then hangs clear
From the cold crystal into the furnace glow
Of ruby and amber lucencies, and dives,
In the brief moment of ten thousand lives
Through fathomless infinities of light,
Then cleansed by lustral flame and frost returns;
And for an instant through my body burns;
The immortal fires of cold-white ecstasy
As down the darkening valley of the night
I keep the old track of mortality.

The old track of mortality is, at least symbolically, the work that lies before us on the physical plane. With each new inspiration perceived in the furnace's glow, we must plunge our talents and skills once more into physical activity, to fully honor the presence and potential of the spark that motivates us.

More Fragments From the Rubáiyát
by Omar Khayyám (as translated by Edward Fitzgerald)

We are no other than a moving row
Of Magic Shadow-shapes that come and go
    Round with the Sun-illumined Lantern held
In Midnight by the Master of the Show.

But helpless Pieces of the Game He plays
Upon this Checker board of Nights and Days;
    Hither and thither moves, and checks, and slays,
And one by one back in the Closet lays.

The Ball no question makes of Ayes and Noes,
But Here or There as strikes the Player goes;
    And he that toss'd you down into the field,
He knows about it all—HE knows—HE knows!

The Moving finger writes; and, having writ,
Moves on: nor all your Piety nor Wit
    Shall lure it back to cancel half a Line,
Nor all your Tears wash out a line of it.

Yesterday This Day's Madness did prepare;
Tomorrow's Silence, Triumph, or Despair:
    Drink! for you know not whence you came, nor why:
Drink! for you know not why you go, nor where.

And this I know: whether the one True Light
Kindle to Love, or Wrath-consume me quite,
    One flash of It within the Tavern caught
Better than in the Temple lost outright.

Aurora Leigh
by Elizabeth Barrett Browning

(From Book VII, Lines 761 through 894)

Truth, so far, in my book; the truth which draws
Through all things upwards—that a two-fold world
Must go to a perfect cosmos. Natural things
And spiritual—who separates those two
In art, in morals, or the social drift,
Tears up the bond of nature and brings death,
Paints futile pictures, writes unreal verse,
Leads vulgar days, deals ignorantly with men,
Is wrong, in short, at all points. We divide
This apple of life, and cut it through the pips:
The perfect round which fitted Venus' hand
Has perished as utterly as if we ate
Both halves. Without the spiritual, observe,
The natural's impossible—no form,
No motion: without sensuous, spiritual
Is inappreciable—no beauty or power:
And in this twofold sphere the twofold man
(For still the artist is intensely a man)
Holds firmly by the natural, to reach
The spiritual beyond it—fixes still
The type with mortal vision, to pierce through,
With eyes immortal, to the antitype
Some call the ideal, better called the real
And certain to be called so presently
When things shall have their names. Look long enough
On any peasant's face here, coarse and lined,
You'll catch Antinous somewhere in that clay,
As perfect featured as he yearns at Rome

From marble pale with beauty; then persist
And, if your apprehension's competent,
You'll find some fairer angel at his back,
As much exceeding him as he the boor,
And pushing him with empyreal disdain
Forever out of sight. Ay, Carrington
Is glad of such a creed; an artist must,
Who paints a tree, a leaf, a common stone,
With just his hand, and finds it suddenly
A-piece with and conterminous to his soul.
Why else do these things move him, leaf or stone?
The bird's not moved that pecks at a spring-shoot;
Nor yet the horse, before a quarry agraze;
But man, the twofold creature, apprehends
The twofold manner, in and outwardly,
And nothing in the world comes single to him,
A mere itself—cup, column, or candlestick,
All patterns of what shall be in the Mount;
The whole temporal show related royally,
And built up to eterne significance
Through the open arms of God. "There's nothing great
Nor small," has said a poet of our day,*
Whose voice will ring beyond the curfew of eve
And not be thrown out by the matin's bell:
And truly, I reiterate, nothing's small!
No lily-muffled hum of a summer bee,
But finds some coupling with the spinning stars;
No pebble at your foot, but proves a sphere;
No chaffinch, but implies the cherubim;
And (glancing on my own thin, veinèd wrist)
In such a little tremor of the blood

*See page 79, "The Informing Spirit" by Emerson

Poems of Light — 106

The whole strong clamor of a vehement soul
Doth utter itself distinct. Earth's crammed with heaven,
And every common bush afire with God;
But only he who sees, takes off his shoes—
The rest sit round it and pluck blackberries,
And daub their natural faces unaware
More and more from the first similitude.
     Truth, so far, in my book! a truth which draws
From all things upward. I, Aurora, still
Have felt it hound me through the wastes of life
As Jove did Io; and, until that Hand
Shall overtake me wholly and on my head
Lay down its large unfluctuating peace,
The feverish gadfly pricks me up and down.
It must be. Art's the witness of what Is
Behind this show. If this world's show were all,
Then imitation would be all in Art;
There, Jove's hand gripes us! For we stand here, we,
If genuine artists, witnessing for God's
Complete, consummate, undivided work;
That every natural flower which grows on earth
Implies a flower upon the spiritual side,
Substantial, archetypal, all aglow
With blossoming causes—not so far away,
But we, whose spirit-sense is somewhat cleared,
May catch at something of the bloom and breath—
Too vaguely apprehended, consciously or not,
And still transferred to picture, music, verse,
For thrilling audient and beholding soul
By signs and touches which are known to souls.
How known, they know not—why, they cannot find,
So straight call out on genius, say, "A man
Produced this," when much rather they should say
"'Tis insight and he saw this."

                    Thus is Art
Self-magnified in magnifying a truth
Which, fully recognized, would change the world
And shift its morals. If a man could feel,
Not one day, in the artist's ecstasy,
But every day, feast, fast, or working-day,
The spiritual significance burn through
The hieroglyphic of material shows,
Henceforward he would paint the globe with wings,
And reverence fish and fowl, the bull, the tree,
And even his very body as a man—
Which now he counts so vile, that all the towns
Make offal of their daughters for its use,
On summer-nights, when God is sad in heaven
To think what goes on in his recreant world
He made quite other; while that moon He made
To shine there, at the first love's covenant,
Shines still, convictive as a marriage ring
Before adulterous eyes.
                        How sure it is,
That, if we say a true word, instantly
We feel 'tis God's, not ours, and pass it on
Like bread at sacrament we taste and pass
Nor handle for a moment, as indeed
We dared to set up any claim to such!
And I—my poem—let my readers talk.
I'm closer to it—I can speak as well:
I'll say with Romney, that the book is weak,
The range uneven, the points of sight obscure,
The music interrupted.
                       Let us go.
The end of woman (or of man, I think)
Is not a book. Alas, the best of books
Is but a word in Art, which soon grows cramped,

Poems of Light — 108

Stiff, dubious-statured with the weight of years,
And drops an accent or digamma down
Some cranny of unfathomable time,
Beyond the critic's reaching. Art itself,
We've called the larger life, must feel the soul
Live past it. For more's felt than is perceived,
And more's perceived than can be interpreted,
And Love strikes higher with his lambent flame
Than Art can pile the fagots.

> *Great art is meant to open our eyes so that we may see the spiritual world. When this becomes possible, then we shall all understand that earth is crammed with heaven, and every common bush afire with God. We will stop profaning the divine by smearing berries on our faces, and learn to rejoice in His constant presence.*

Synthesis
by Carl Japikse

Every step creates a trace
that must be doubled back.
Thus from one comes
two in hopes some day
of reaching one again.

Lots of friends of mine think
the first step easy, the second, hard.
It's easy for a rock
to fall, much harder
for the same to fly.

But I recall when even rocks
found falling tough. The updraft
kept on sweeping
them away like
swiftly swirling snow.

O my friends, I've walked
a measured line, sometimes
leaning to the right, sometimes to the left.
And there were days I
leaned both ways at once.

Last week I found
for one brief second
I didn't lean at all; I stood
in hopeful rhythm,
and took that second step.

Death

Other than romantic love, few topics have had a greater monopoly on the minds of poets than death. Some poets, like John Donne and John Keats, were almost obsessed with the subject. But death was a much more fearsome prospect in their days, when the average life span ended in the 30's.

For all the poems about death, however, there are surprisingly few that actually get beyond the superficial aspects of the subject and touch the light behind the experience. Most dwell on the impact of death on those remaining, and seek to provide comfort for those who mourn.

I have tried to collect those poems that go a step further and endeavor to reveal the truth about death and the cyclic nature of the principle of divine rebirth. In reading about life after death, it is necessary to distinguish between theology, which is speculation by people who admit that they have no direct experience to guide them, and the intuition, which enables us to perceive the realities of death directly, objectively.

The Unknown Region
by Walt Whitman

Darest thou now, O Soul,
Walk out with me toward the Unknown Region,
Where neither ground is for the feet, nor any path
    to follow?

No map, there, nor guide,
Nor voice sounding, nor touch of human hand,
Nor face with blooming flesh, nor lips, nor eyes,
    are in that land.

I know it not, O Soul;
Nor dost thou, all is a blank before us—
All waits, undreamed of, in that region—that
    inaccessible land.

Till, when the tie is loosened,
All but the ties eternal, Time and Space,
Nor darkness, gravitation, sense, nor any bounds
    bound us.

Then we burst forth, we float,
In Time and Space, O Soul! prepared for them;
Equal, equipped at last (O joy! O fruit of all) them to
    fulfill, O, Soul!

Can This Be Death?
by Alexander Pope

Vital spark of heavenly flame!
Quit, O quit this mortal frame:
    Trembling, hoping, lingering, flying,
    O the pain, the bliss of dying!
Cease, fond Nature, cease thy strife,
And let me languish into life.

    Hark! they whisper; angels say,
    Sister Spirit, come away!
    What is this absorbs me quite?
    Steals my senses, shuts my sight,
Drowns my spirits, draws my breath,
Tell me, O soul, can this be death?

The world recedes; it disappears!
Heav'n opens on my eyes, my ears
    With sounds seraphic ring!
Lend, lend your wings! I mount! I fly!
O Grave, where is thy victory?
    O Death! where is thy sting?

After Death in Arabia
by Edwin Arnold

He who died at Azan sends
This to comfort all his friends:

Faithful friends! It lies, I know
Pale and white and cold as snow;
And ye say, "Abdallah's dead!"
Weeping at the feet and head.
I can see your falling tears,
I can hear your sighs and prayers;
Yet I smile and whisper this:
"I am not the thing you kiss;
Cease your tears and let it lie;
It *was* mine—it is not I."

Sweet Friends! What the women lave
For its last bed in the grave,
Is a tent which I am quitting,
Is a garment no more fitting,
Is a cage, from which at last,
Like a hawk, my soul hath passed.
Love the inmate, not the room—
The wearer, not the garb; the plume
Of the falcon, not the bars
That kept him from these splendid stars!

Loving friends! be wise, and dry
Straightway every weeping eye.
What ye lift upon the bier
Is not worth a wistful tear.
'Tis an empty sea shell—one
Out of which the pearl is gone;

Poems of Light — 114

The shell is broken, it lies there;
The pearl, the all, the soul, is here.
'Tis an earthen jar, whose lid
Allah sealed, the while it hid
That treasure of his treasury,
A mind that loved him; let it lie!
Let the shard be the earth's once more,
Since the gold shines in his store!

Allah glorious! Allah good!
Now thy world is understood;
Now the long, long wonder ends!
Yet ye weep, my erring friends,
While the man whom ye call dead,
In unspoken bliss, instead,
Lives and loves you; lost, 'tis true,
By such light as shines for you;
But in light you cannot see
Of unfulfilled felicity—
In enlarging paradise,
Lives a life that never dies.

Farewell, friends, yet not farewell;
Where I am ye too shall dwell.
I am gone before your face,
A moment's time, a little space.
When ye come where I have stepped,
Ye will wonder why ye wept;
Yet will know by wise love taught,
That here is all and there is naught.
Weep a while, if ye are fain,
Sunshine still must follow rain;
Only not at death—for death,
Now I know, is that first breath

Which our souls draw when we enter
Life, which is of all life center.

Be ye certain all seems love,
Viewed from Allah's throne above;
Be ye stout of heart and come,
Bravely onward to your home!
La Allah illa Allah! yea!
Thou love divine, thou love alway!

He who died at Azan gave
This to those who made his grave.

The moment of death is actually an instant of great joy for the soul, as it marks the completion of another creative project—another life on earth. Instead of fearing death, we should accept it gracefully when it occurs—even in others— and try to share in the wonderful essence of joy that fills the soul. It is almost barbaric to grieve excessively. Grief estranges us from the one we miss.

Poems of Light — 116

Under the Light
by Emily Dickinson

Under the light, yet under,
Under the Grass and the Dirt.
Under the Beetle's Cellar
Under the Clover's Root,

Further than Arm could stretch
Were it Giant long,
Further than Sunshine could
Were the Day Year long.

Over the Light, yet over,
Over the Arc of the Bird—
Over the Comet's chimney,
Over the Cubit's Head.

Further than Guess can gallop
Further than Riddle ride—
Oh for a Disc to the Distance
Between Ourselves and the Dead!

Sevens
by Carl Japikse

When I am dust
conform I must.

When I am sand
I brush your hand.

When I'm the sea
I set you free.

When I am air
I'm everywhere.

When I am fire
I will expire.

When I am rain
I live again.

When I am light...
but I'm not quite.

Ozymandias
by Percy Bysshe Shelley

I met a traveler from an antique land
Who said: Two vast and trunkless legs of stone
Stand in a desert. Near them, on the sand,
Half sunk, a shattered visage lies, whose frown,
And wrinkled lip, and sneer of cold command,
Tell that its sculptor well those passions read
Which yet survive, stamped on these lifeless things,
The hand that mocked them and the heart that fed;
And on the pedestal these words appear:
"My name is Ozymandias, king of kings:
Look on my works, ye Mighty, and despair!"
Nothing beside remains. Round the decay
Of that colossal wreck, boundless and bare
The lone and level sands stretch far away.

Sail Out For Good, Eidólon Yacht!
by Walt Whitman

Heave the anchor short!
Raise main-sail and jib—steer forth,
O little white-hull'd sloop, now speed on really deep
　　waters,
(I will not call it our concluding voyage,
But outset and sure entrance to the truest, best,
　　maturest);
Depart, depart from solid earth—no more returning to
　　these shores,
Now on for aye our infinite free venture wending,
Spurning all yet tried ports, seas, hawsers, densities,
　　gravitation,
Sail out for good eidólon yacht of me!

Rima

by Gustavo Adolfo Bécquer (translated by Carl Japikse)

Abandoned by its owner,
The harp leans 'gainst the wall,
Gathering dust and silence
Within the concert hall.

What music must dwell in its strings,
Unheard in the shadows of night,
Like a bird asleep on a branch,
Waiting to be aroused to flight!

Ay! thought I. How often does genius
Lie asleep, upon the hearth of the soul,
Like Lazarus, needing a voice to call—
"Rise up, go forth, be whole!"

The Windhover
by Gerard Manley Hopkins

To Christ Our Lord

I caught this morning morning's minion, king-
    dom of daylight's dauphin, dapple-dawn-drawn
        Falcon, in his riding
    Of the rolling level underneath him steady air,
        and striding
High there, how he rung upon the rein of a wimpling wing
In his ecstasy! then off, off forth on swing,
    As a skate's heel sweeps smooth on a bow-bend:
        the hurl and gliding
    Rebuffed the big wind. My heart in hiding
Stirred for a bird—the achieve of, the mastery of the thing!

Brute beauty and valour and act, oh, air, pride, plume,
        here
    Buckle! And the fire that breaks from thee then,
        a billion
Times told lovelier, more dangerous. O my chevalier!

    No wonder of it: sheer plod makes plough down
        sillion
Shine, and blue-bleak embers, ah my dear,
    Fall, gall themselves, and gash gold-vermilion.

Death
by Emily Dickinson

Death is a dialogue between
The spirit and the dust.
"Dissolve," says Death; the spirit, "Sir,
I have another trust."

Death doubts it, argues from the ground,
The spirit turns away,
Just laying off, for evidence,
An overcoat of clay.

Joy, Shipmate, Joy!
by Walt Whitman

Joy, shipmate, joy!
(Pleas'd to my soul at death I cry),
Our life is closed, our life begins,
The long, long anchorage we leave,
The ship is clear at last, she leaps!
She swiftly courses from the shore,
Joy, shipmate, joy!

Visions

Every now and then, a poet gets swept up into the abstract realms of inspiration and has a vision of what life means. It might be the vision of John Keats when first looking into Chapman's translation of Homer—or the vision of William Wordsworth as a child remembering earlier lives. The important thing is to realize how much these visions enrich our human life and understanding.

You may be one of those people who yearn to be rich. If so, I wish you luck in your quest. But keep in mind that even if you reach your goal, you will only have a few years to enjoy it. The summer home, the luxury cars, the yacht—these are toys to play with in our declining years. You can't take them with you.

How much more valuable is spiritual vision! It gives us strength of heart, a sense of direction, a measure of wisdom, and peace. They need no insurance, for they cannot be stolen. They need no guarantees, for they never fail. And they can, indeed, be taken from life to life.

If poetry has a purpose—and it does—it is to be the spiritual eyes for mankind. Poetry tries to capture a glimpse of the vision and share it for the benefit of all. Here are some fragments of that vision.

Here on Earth
by Carl Japikse

The oddest thing
about the earth
is half the time
is spent at night.

Like stars that
never rise nor set
the day is fixed
and can't be changed.

Yet some of us
feel out of step
and from the earth
have grown estranged.

O, come with me
and see my world,
where all of time
is hung in light.

On First Looking Into Chapman's Homer
by John Keats

Much have I travell'd in the realms of gold,
    And many goodly states and kingdoms seen;
    Round many western islands have I been
Which bards in fealty to Apollo hold.
Oft of one wide expanse had I been told
    That deep-brow'd Homer ruled as his demesne;
    Yet did I never breathe its pure serene
Till I heard Chapman speak out loud and bold:
Then felt I like some watcher of the skies
    When a new planet swims into his ken;
Or like stout Cortez when with eagle eyes
    He star'd at the Pacific—and all his men
Look'd at each other with a wild surmise—
    Silent, upon a peak in Darien.

Dirt
by Robert Service

Dirt is just matter out of place,
    So scientists aver;
But when I see a miner's face
    I wonder if they err.
For grit and grime and grease may be
    In God's constructive plan,
A symbol of nobility,
    The measure of a man.

There's nought so clean as honest dirt,
    So of its worth I sing;
I value more an oily shirt
    Than garment of a king.
There's nought so proud as honest sweat,
    And though its stink we cuss,
We kid-glove chaps are in the debt
    Of those who sweat for us.

It's dirt and sweat that make us folks
    Proud as we are today;
We owe our wealth to weary blokes
    Befouled by soot and clay.
And where you see a belly fat
    A dozen more are lean...
By God! I'd sooner doff my hat
    To washer-wife than queen.

So here's a song to dirt and sweat,
    A grace to grit and grime;

Poems of Light — 128

A hail to workers who beget
    The wonders of our time.
And as they gaze, through gutter-girt,
    To palaces enskied,
Let them believe, by sweat and dirt,
    They, too, are glorified.

The most helpful vision you can have is a sense of the value of the work you are involved in, whether or not a paycheck is involved. If you can approach your work with cheerfulness and a sense of nobility, you will have found one of the great secrets of life. And that will set the stage for even greater visions of what you can be.

The Clod and the Pebble
by William Blake

Love seeketh not Itself to please,
Nor for itself hath any care;
But for another gives its ease,
And builds a Heaven in Hell's despair.

    So sang a little Clod of Clay,
    Trodden with the cattle's feet:
    But a Pebble of the brook,
    Warbled out these metres meet.

Love seeketh only Self to please,
To bind another to Its delight:
Joys in another's loss of ease,
And builds a Hell in Heaven's despite.

We are busy building one or the other, here on earth—either heaven or hell. If we strive to express divine love impersonally, we will build heaven; but if we try to distort love to serve our selfish needs, we will have a thorough taste of hell before we're through.

Ode
by William Wordsworth

(Intimations of Immortality from Recollections of Early Childhood)

  The Child is Father of the Man;
  And I could wish my days to be
  Bound each to each by natural piety.

I.
There was a time when meadow, grove, and stream,
The earth, and every common sight,
  To me did seem
  Apparelled in celestial light,
The glory and the freshness of a dream.
It is not now as it hath been of yore—
  Turn whereso'er I may,
   By night or day,
The things which I have seen I now can see no more.

II.
  The Rainbow comes and goes,
  And lovely is the Rose,
  The Moon doth with delight
Look round her when the heavens are bare,
  Waters on a starry night
  Are beautiful and fair;
  The sunshine is a glorious birth;
  But yet I know, where'er I go,
That there hath past away a glory from the earth.

III.
Now, while the birds thus sing a joyous song,
    And while the young lambs bound
        As to the tabor's sound,
To me alone there came a thought of grief:
A timely utterance gave that thought relief,
    And I again am strong:
The cataracts blow their trumpets from the steep;
No more shall grief of mine the season wrong;
I hear the Echoes through the mountains throng,
The Winds come to me from the fields of sleep,
    And all the earth is gay;
        Land and sea
    Give up themselves to jollity,
      And with the heart of May
    Doth every Beast keep holiday—
        Thou Child of Joy,
Shout round me, let me hear thy shouts, thou happy
    Shepherd-boy!

IV.
Ye blessèd Creatures, I have heard the call
    Ye to each other make; I see
The heavens laugh with you in your jubilee;
    My heart is at your festival,
      My head hath its coronal,
The fulness of your bliss, I feel—I feel it all.
        Oh evil day! if I were sullen
          While Earth herself is adorning,
            This sweet May-morning,
         And the Children are culling
            On every side,
      In a thousand valleys far and wide,
      Fresh flowers; while the sun shines warm,

And the Babe leaps up on his Mother's arm:
        I hear, I hear, with joy I hear!
    —But there's a Tree, of many, one,
A single field which I have looked upon,
Both of them speak of something that is gone:
        The Pansy at my feet
        Doth the same tale repeat:
Whither is fled the visionary gleam?
Where is it now, the glory and the dream?

V

Our birth is but a sleep and a forgetting:
The Soul that rises with us, our life's Star,
        Hath had elsewhere its setting,
        And cometh from afar:
    Not in entire forgetfulness,
    And not in utter nakedness,
But trailing clouds of glory do we come
        From God, who is our home:
Heaven lies about us in our infancy!
Shades of the prison-house begin to close
        Upon the growing Boy,
But He beholds the light, and whence it flows,
        He sees it in his joy;
The Youth, who daily farther from the east
        Must travel, still is Nature's Priest,
        And by the vision splendid
        Is on his way attended;
At length the Man perceives it die away,
And fade into the light of common day.

VI

Earth fills her lap with pleasures of her own;
Yearnings she hath in her own natural kind,
And, even with something of a Mother's mind,
    And no unworthy aim,
  The homely Nurse doth all she can
To make her Foster-child, her Inmate Man,
    Forget the glories he hath known,
And that imperial palace whence he came.

VII

Behold the Child among his newborn blisses,
A six years' Darling of a pigmy size!
See, where 'mid work of his own hand he lies,
Fretted by sallies of his mother's kisses,
With light upon him from his father's eyes!
See, at his feet, some little plan or chart,
Some fragment from his dream of human life,
Shaped by himself with newly-learned art;
    A wedding or a festival,
    A mourning or a funeral;
      And this hath now his heart,
    And unto this he frames his song:
      Then will he fit his tongue
To dialogues of business, love, or strife;
    But it will not be long
    Ere this be thrown aside,
    And with new joy and pride
The little Actor cons another part;
Filling from time to time his "humorous stage"
With all the Persons, down to palsied Age,
That Life brings with her in her equipage;
    As if his whole vocation
    Were endless imitation.

VIII

Thou, whose exterior semblance doth belie
    Thy Soul's Immensity;
Thou best Philosopher, who yet dost keep
Thy heritage, thou Eye among the blind,
That, deaf and silent, read'st the eternal deep,
Haunted for ever by the eternal mind—
    Mighty Prophet! Seer blest!
    On whom those truths do rest,
Which we are toiling all our lives to find,
In darkness lost, the darkness of the grave;
Thou, over whom thy Immortality
Broods like the Day, a Master o'er a Slave,
A Presence which is not to be put by;
Thou little Child, yet glorious in the might
Of heaven-born freedom on thy Being's height,
Why with such earnest pains dost thou provoke
The years to bring the inevitable yoke,
Thus blindly with thy blessedness at strife?
Full soon thy Soul shall have her earthly freight,
And custom lie upon thee with a weight,
Heavy as frost, and deep almost as life!

IX

    O joy! that in our embers
    Is something that doth live,
    That nature yet remembers
    What was so fugitive!
The thought of our past years in me doth breed
Perpetual benediction: not indeed
For that which is most worthy to be blest;
Delight and liberty, the simple creed
Of Childhood, whether busy or at rest,
With new-fledged hope still fluttering in his breast:

		Not for these I raise
		The songs of thanks and praise;
	But for those obstinate questionings
	Of sense and outward things,
	Fallings from us, vanishings;
	Blank misgivings of a Creature
Moving about in worlds not realised,
High instincts before which our mortal Nature
Did tremble like a guilty Thing surprised:
		But for those first affections,
		Those shadowy recollections,
	Which, be they what they may,
Are yet the fountain-light of all our day,
Are yet a master-light of all our seeing;
	Uphold us, cherish, and have power to make
Our noisy years seem moments in the being
Of the eternal Silence: truths that wake,
			To perish never:
Which neither listlessness, nor mad endeavour,
		Nor Man nor Boy,
Nor all that is an enmity with joy,
Can utterly abolish or destroy!
	Hence in a season of calm weather
		Though inland far we be,
Our Souls have sight of that immortal sea
		Which brought us hither,
	Can in a moment travel thither,
And see the Children sport upon the shore,
And hear the mighty waters rolling evermore.

X

Then sing, ye Birds, sing, sing a joyous song!
    And let the young Lambs bound
    As to the tabor's sound!
We in thought will join your throng,
    Ye that pipe and ye that play,
    Ye that through your hearts today
    Feel the gladness of the May!
What though the radiance which was once so bright
Be now for ever taken from my sight,
    Though nothing can bring back the hour
Of splendour in the grass, of glory in the flower;
    We will grieve not, rather find
    Strength in what remains behind;
    In the primal sympathy
    Which having been must ever be;
    In the soothing thoughts that spring
    Out of human suffering;
    In the faith that looks through death,
In years that bring the philosophic mind.

XI

And O, ye Fountains, Meadows, Hills, and Groves,
Forebode not any severing of our loves!
Yet in my heart of hearts I feel your might;
I only have relinquished one delight
To live beneath your more habitual sway.
I love the Brooks which down their channels fret,
Even more than when I tripped lightly as they;
The innocent brightness of a newborn Day
    Is lovely yet;
The Clouds that gather round the setting sun
Do take a sober colouring from an eye
That hath kept watch o'er man's mortality;

Another race hath been, and other palms are won.
Thanks to the human heart by which we live,
Thanks to its tenderness, its joys, and fears,
To me the meanest flower that blows can give
Thoughts that do often lie too deep for tears.

Koh-i-Noor
by Carl Japikse

We move throughout our lives like blinded peacocks
Pecking for the diamond in the rocks,
But finding only flint for Afghan's highest throne,
While passion drags us downward into stone.

And as we strut our cadenced stroll through hell,
Feathering out our plumage like a shell,
Believing paste to be the sign of power—
Aurangzeb's mountain fades within the tower!

As monuments we stand, with jewels in our crowns;
But monuments to what—to joys or frowns?
The Koh-i-Noor is worthless, hidden in the dark;
Ill luck attends whoever veils its spark.

The Koh-i-Noor—"mountain of light"—is one of the most famous diamonds in the world. Once the eye of the famed peacock throne of Afghanistan, it represents here the dual nature of our aspiration. Do we seek might—or light? Is our life a monument to God—or to materialism?

The World's All Right
by Robert Service

Be honest, kindly, simple, true;
Seek good in all, scorn but pretence;
Whatever sorrow comes to you,
Believe in Life's Beneficence!

The World's all right; serene I sit
And cease to puzzle over it.
There's much that's mighty strange, no doubt;
But Nature knows what she's about;
And in a million years or so
We'll know more than today we know.
Old Evolution's under way—
    What ho! the World's all right, I say.

Could things be other than they are?
All's in its place, from mote to star.
The thistledown that flits and flies
Could drift no hair-breadth otherwise.
What is, must be; with rhythmic laws
All Nature chimes, Effect and Cause.
The sand-grain and the sun obey—
    What ho! the World's all right, I say.

Just try to get the Cosmic touch,
The sense that "you" don't matter much.
A million stars are in the sky;
A million planets plunge and die;
A million million men are sped;
A million million wait ahead.

Each plays his part and has his day—
    What ho! the World's all right, I say.

Just try to get the Chemic view:
A million million lives made "you."
In lives a million you will be
Immortal down Eternity;
Immortal on this earth to range,
With never death, but ever change.
You always were, and will be aye—
    What ho! the World's all right, I say.

Be glad! And do not blindly grope
For Truth that lies beyond our scope:
A sober plot informeth all
Of Life's uproarious carnival.
Your day is such a little one,
A gnat that lives from sun to sun;
Yet gnat and you have parts to play—
    What ho! the World's all right, I say.

And though it's written from the start,
Just act your best your little part.
Just be as happy as you can,
And serve your kind, and die—a man.
Just live the good that in you lies,
And seek no guerdon from the skies;
Just make your Heaven here, today—
    What ho! the World's all right, I say.

Remember! in Creation's swing
The Race and not the man's the thing.
There's battle, murder, sudden death,
And pestilence, with poisoned breath.

Yet quick forgotten are such woes;
On, on the stream of Being flows.
Truth, Beauty, Love uphold their sway—
    What ho! the World's all right, I say.

The World's all right; serene I sit,
And joy that I am part of it;
And put my trust in Nature's plan,
And try to aid her all I can;
Content to pass, if in my place
I've served the uplift of the Race.
Truth! Beauty! Love! O Radiant Day—
    What ho! the World's all right, I say.

The Divine Image
by William Blake

To Mercy, Pity, Peace, and Love,
All pray in their distress:
And to these virtues of delight
Return their thankfulness.

For Mercy, Pity, Peace, and Love,
Is God our father dear:
And Mercy, Pity, Peace, and Love,
Is Man his child and care.

For Mercy has a human heart;
Pity, a human face;
And Love, the human form divine;
And Peace, the human dress.

Then every man of every clime
That prays in his distress
Prays to the human form divine
Love, Mercy, Pity, Peace.

And all must love the human form,
In heathen, Turk, or Jew.
Where Mercy, Love, and Pity dwell,
There God is dwelling, too.

Heaven is not some remote place; it can be found within our minds and hearts, if these be filled with Love, Mercy, Pity, and Peace.

The Base of All Metaphysics
by Walt Whitman

And now gentlemen,
A word I give to remain in your memories and minds,
As base and finalè too for all metaphysics.

(So to the students the old professor,
At the close of his crowded course).

Having studied the new and antique, the Greek and
    Germanic systems,
Kant having studied and stated, Fichte and Schelling
    and Hegel,
Stated the lore of Plato, and Socrates greater than Plato,
And greater than Socrates sought and stated,
    Christ divine having studied long,
I see reminiscent today those Greek and Germanic
    systems,
See the philosophies all, Christian churches and tenets see,
Yet underneath Socrates clearly see, and underneath
    Christ the divine I see,
The dear love of man for his comrade, the attraction of
    friend to friend,
Of the well-married husband and wife, of children
    and parents,
Of city for city and land for land.

Renewal
by Carl Japikse

She smiles with joy and knows her travail's through;
The babe has come, and night has turned to morn.
This birth of one has been the birth of two:
For with the child, a mother has been born.
    Within her heart shines forth a hidden light,
    Preserved long years to be revealed this night.

Stirred by fresh hopes, the light within her grows:
The light of love, a treasure undefiled.
In purest colors, from the heart it flows,
And like a prayer, enwraps the sleeping child.
    Such love transforms the life of man to art:
    It speaks with fullness from the mother's heart.

No wise men come, no shepherds in the field;
Still, angels tend the mother's every need.
She knows not what the passing years will yield,
But trusts in light, the life within the seed.
    And so, a mother's faith all hopes renew;
    This babe of hers shall be a Christ child, too.